EXERCISE YOUR
ASK MUSCLE

*The No-Weight Workout with
Proven Results*

By
Nancy Dunleavy

Exercise Your Ask Muscle
The No-Weight Workout with Proven Results
By **Nancy Dunleavy**

ISBN-10:1-942489-17-X
ISBN-13:978-1-942489-17-7

Acknowledgements

Gratitude is something that has enriched my life in innumerable ways. I've learned that there really is strength in words and one of the easiest but most powerful things that a person can say is 'Thank you'. Whether the thanks is for a gift, a service, encouragement offered or even constructive criticism received– I have found that gratitude is the gift that keeps on giving. So, in that spirit of giving, I would like to say 'thank you' to the many people who helped to shape this book. Both with their stories and their insight.

I am grateful for the people who helped me prove this concept—they willingly took time out of their busy days to sit down with us, sharing their stories and allowing us to capture their experiences as evidence for this book. Susan McDonald, Michelle

Tepper, Jennifer Sandusky, Fallyn Flaherty-Earp, Kim Rivera, Regina Rinehimer, Shannon Power, Larissa Polejaev, and Claire Costello. Your generosity truly overwhelms me!

I am equally grateful to the many connectors who have shared their stories with me via email. Among these, Meggin (Forti) DeBarberie, Stephanie McCullough, Erin Bushnell, Kristina L. Wahl, Cristina A. Hug, Ellen Fisher, and Mike Witowski. Through your generous gift of time you've helped me to validate the role of a connector!

A huge 'THANK YOU' to Malcom Gladwell and Bob Burg, both giants in this field whose work has inspired me and whose writings have paved the way for like-minded individuals to understand the contributions that "connectors" can make. And, to Liz Dow, whose endeavor to link connector behaviors to leadership lessons resulted in the original list of 'Philadelphia's Top 101 Connectors' in 2006. Your vision and encouragement have helped to shape my life's journey in a profound way.

My gratitude circle would not be complete without acknowledging the enormous encouragement (and nagging) of two friends in particular—Sue Schick who was in the audience the day it all began and has encouraged my speaking career and, my dearest friend of 3 decades, Terri Donohue who has invested deeply in helping me to bring this book to life. I consider her the most loyal of midwives helping me to "birth" this publication.

To my Dunleavy team colleagues, I am grateful, every day, that God put you in my path, exactly the day I needed you to be there. You're simply the best! It is with a very full heart that I acknowledge the gifts you've given me to complete this work. In addition to the latitude to devote the time needed to take on speaking engagements to share the connector story you've also sacrificed by allowing me to have Adrienne's talent, time and focus dedicated to moving the work forward as my publication partner. Adrienne Murray, you have an incredible talent and lots of energy for writing, evidence working on 2 books at once! I so appreciate the gentleness of your (firm) nudging when procrastination took over and I will forever be grateful for how your inspired "fable" wove it all together!

And, finally—immeasurable gratitude for my dear family. Those whose blood I share and those whose families I have been welcomed to. My husband Michael, who I love so much, has been my partner, confidant and cheerleader—always the first to urge me to follow what's in my heart, even when he doesn't quite know how it will impact him! Thank you, hon. My brothers, Harry and Tom, who are the source of lifetime joy to me—I'm so proud of you as fathers, leaders and friends. Their wives, Lynne and Jennifer—I could not love you more if you were my sisters, and to my nieces and nephews, gratitude for all that each of you brings to me and the world. This book is really for you— learn these lessons early and exercise them often. Brittany, Matthew, Luke, Jesse and Isabella—if you choose to embrace these concepts I promise that you will find that it's in giving that we truly receive.

Table of Contents

Introduction

It's funny; when you're young, you're given such mixed messages about asking for help. When you made a mess, you'd be asked, "Why didn't you ask me for help?" When you struggled and the adults around you saw the value in working things out on your own, you were told, "Don't ask me; you try it first."

Then there are the extremes. Adults in your life may never have helped with anything. Maybe they were absent, maybe they didn't care, or maybe they had simply learned that way. Perhaps your adults did everything for you before you even asked, never letting you learn lessons on your own.

Some studies suggest that your personality is mostly set by the time you reach first grade, meaning that the lessons you learned on the playground and around the dinner table have a huge impact on who you are right now and on how you handle circumstances in your life.

I'm here to tell you that new lessons can be learned, and, if you are very intentional about how you live your life, you can exercise a muscle that is oftentimes greatly out of shape: your "Ask" muscle. Yes, I said Ask. Your Ask muscle is just as valuable as any other muscle you may work out at the gym—maybe even more valuable, if you ask me. Why? Because I have seen it time and time again propel people from where they are to where they want to be.

I believe in the power of the "connector." A connector is someone who seems to know everyone and is able to zero in on the needs of one person and connect them to another who can meet that need. You may have heard of this person in the writings of Malcolm Gladwell, Bob Burg, and Liz Dow. I happen to be a connector, and in fact I was voted one of Philadelphia's top 101 connectors in 2006. When people asked me what was the "secret in my sauce," I set about finding out what was different about how I do what I do. And if you know anything about a connector, you know that we like to share. Since then, I've been letting people everywhere, in every walk of life, in on my secret.

What I found that a connector possesses is actually a very well-developed Ask muscle. How will we know whom to connect to if we aren't asked? How will we know what people need if we don't ask them? How will we get our own needs met if we don't speak up?

You may think it's too easy just to ask for something and get it, right? Wrong! I have dozens of stories to prove to you that it's not, but we'll get to those later. For now, I would like to share a fable with you that will *show* you how to do what I do. The fable is the work of a gifted writer, Adrienne Murray, who also happens to be my colleague in the company. I marvel at her ability to take a concept like this and turn it into a wonderful story. So sit back, relax, and enjoy the read.

Winning by Losing
A Fable by Adrienne Murray

Everything faded to black, and her heart pounded in her ears. She was sure her face was red, and she could feel beads of sweat forming on the back of her neck. How could she have lost the account? She'd had it in the bag. She'd done her due diligence. She had shut herself away from the world and dug into the research. It's what she'd always done in the past. And it always worked. Although, if she was honest with herself, this was happening more and more often.

She gathered her bag and trench coat, smiled at the sympathetic faces around her, and walked out the door of the boardroom. She was able to wave off the talkative lady at the front desk, saying, "Have a great day, I'm in a rush. Don't want to miss my flight." The cadence of her words went up at the end of the sentence in a singsong kind of way, hoping this would hide the quiver in her voice.

The fact that she had to walk right past her competition when she left the office was the icing on top of a rather tasteless cake. Before this meeting, Miranda Morris hadn't even known she had competition, let alone this guy. But Dallas, Texas, wasn't her normal market. Maybe he was a local with the inside track? Whatever the case, the ease of the smile on his face irritated her. Let him smile, she thought. I didn't want to have to come halfway across the country for a client, anyway.

Miranda held her head high and threw her shoulders back when she walked past him—right until the heel of her shoe caught on the edge of a throw rug. Like a clumsy newborn calf, her ankles wobbled and bent as she struggled to stay upright. She was able to catch the expletives that rumbled up her throat before they made it out of her mouth. Thank God for small favors, she thought.

And who was there to catch her? Smiley Pete, of course. If she hadn't been so embarrassed, she would have seen the way he tried to help her maintain some dignity, placing his hand gently on her elbow to help further stop her fall. "Happens to me all of the time," he said with that same grin on his face.

She took a deep breath. "Thank you. I'm in a hurry. Don't want to miss my flight."

Smiley removed his hand from her elbow and placed his finger to his temple, giving a simple salute. Miranda turned her watery eyes forward and walked out the enormous glass doors. The farther from the suite of offices she got, the more she could feel her temperature regulating. Taking several more deep breaths helped a bit to steady her nerves. "Just put one foot in front of the other and get the hell outta here" became her mantra.

Those words played over and over in her head all the way downstairs and to the awaiting car. Stepping into the drizzle, Miranda breathed in the moist air and took care, watching where she stepped. Her driver smiled at her while he ran around the car to grab her bag. She didn't wait for him to open the door but opened it herself. She rarely let anyone open a door for her.

Once in the car, she allowed herself to think. Where had she gone wrong? At her home office in Charlotte, North Carolina, she had a bevy of colleagues who had worked hard for this moment. Actually, not this exact moment, where she sat feeling dejected and like a fraud in a private car. The moment that she and her colleagues had planned so well for was when she walked in and wowed the client with her knowledge and then walked out after the shaking of hands and the client putting his signature on the well-crafted contract. *That* was the moment she and her colleagues had been working for. So many hours completely wasted.

Sitting back and settling in for the ride to the airport, Miranda reflected on the last twenty-four hours. She had flown into Dallas-Fort Worth around 3:30 in the afternoon the day before. She remembered the feeling of butterflies in her stomach. This one meeting could have helped launch her company from a small enterprise to one with national reach— unchartered waters for her and her staff.

Presently, her boutique consulting firm serviced up-and-coming corporations in North Carolina. And one client in Virginia, but that didn't really count in her mind. The client was her brother, Simon. He had hired her, most likely because he loved her, at the onset of her business. Her firm had grown so much larger though and, truth be told, had really outgrown his small printing company. She did think it was sweet when he asked about her business and if there was any way he could help. She wished he could, but she was in the big leagues now. And what she was trying to grasp was way out of his reach.

This one though, Masterson Technologies, would have thrust them into an untapped market. She had the people who could do the job. She knew the talent she employed and trusted her staff and her gut. This had such potential. And then *poof*, it was gone.

She remembered landing yesterday and sending a text to her partner, "Just landed, wish me luck!" She put an airplane emoji next to the "just landed" part—it was safe to say she was excited. She walked off the plane and made her way to the baggage claim department, where she found the man with the sign for her private car. Yes, private car. The little girl who once had to wear hand-me-downs from her sister who was ten years older was in her own private car.

She was too nervous and, honestly, too self-absorbed to make small talk with her driver during the ride from the airport to the hotel. After she climbed out of the car and tipped the driver, a pleasant little fellow opened the door to the hotel. If she had been in her element, she would have said hello and maybe even given him a tip for his service. But she was neither in her element nor thinking about being pleasant to the doorman. Sorry, no tip fella.

The lobby was a blur and Miranda sped past the front desk, although she did remember checking in.

The room was what she expected, nothing more and nothing less. She methodically took clothes from her bag and hung them in the closet, making note to shake and separate the suit she had chosen specifically for tomorrow's pitch.

Hunkering down for the night, she read and reread her proposal for the next day. The room was not too hot or too cold. Actually, no air moved at all, which can sometimes be worse than anything else. She had a fitful night's sleep, to say the least.

Miranda awoke before her alarm sounded. She dressed for the day and prepared herself as best as she could. She looked over the copious amount of notes that she and her colleagues had taken. Gathering her bags and materials, Miranda made a mental note of everything she had brought with her and everything she carried out as she left the room. Satisfied, she left, hearing the door click loudly behind her. She breezed past the front desk again. She did not want to be late and had no time for chitchat.

In the imposing building that housed the headquarters of Masterson's, Miranda's mind was three steps ahead of her feet. Without really looking at the security guard, she asked for admittance to the tenth floor. When she entered the offices, the annoyingly chatty receptionist greeted her. She asked Miranda to take a seat. "Would you like a glass of water? How about a scone? Where are you from? When do you leave?" So many questions, and Miranda did not have patience for any of them. Thank God the man sitting in the corner with the giant grin picked up the conversation with the receptionist. As for Miranda, she was ready for the presentation…ready for the "kill."

From the looks on the partners' faces, she knew they were impressed. She told them what she and her firm could do for them. She showed them the benefits of going with her company. In her mind's eye, it was like watching a well-choreographed dance. She spun and twirled, dipped and bowed. They clapped and gave a standing ovation—at least, that's what was supposed to have happened. But it didn't.

She gave her best pitch and they politely thanked her. They were impressed and even told her so. But, "You see," the head honcho said, "we got a last minute recommendation and it was down to the two of you. We've decided to go with…" She couldn't remember the name. Didn't care to, really. But she knew it was Smiley Pete from the lobby.

She was crushed but did her best to give herself an internal pep talk. Well, she thought, what's done is done. She would fly home. She would face her colleagues and look for the next big thing. But this account would have been phenomenal.

Miranda hung her head and closed her eyes, trying to stop the thoughts that swirled around in her mind and forced her back to her glum reality. Soon enough, the car pulled in front of the airport. Miranda slid out of her seat and accepted her bag from the driver's hand. "Thanks," she mumbled as she slipped a tip into his hand. She was only vaguely familiar with Dallas-Fort Worth Airport but found her gate easily enough. She normally flew nonstop but, adding insult to the injury of this trip, the few nonstops from DFW to Charlotte were booked.

The slow drizzle had turned into a sheet of rain by the time Miranda sat down in her departure area. Wind buffeted the rain against the window, so much so that she could barely see the lights outside on the tarmac. That's when the ten-minute delay sign flashed next to her flight number. The older lady sitting next to her leaned over and said, "I don't know if I'll make my connecting flight. I'm going home to Charlotte from Atlanta."

Miranda's head jolted up. "I'm heading the same way. Why do you think you may not make the connection?"

"Oh honey," the woman said, "if you're on the same plane, that layover is only forty minutes. And that airport is huge." The woman shook her head and fumbled with her phone, presumably calling her ride to explain the possible delay.

Miranda shook her head in disbelief and looked at her ticket. Sure enough, a forty-minute layover. Perfect. Could this day get any worse? she wondered. Mercifully, as the minutes ticked slowly by, the clouds began to break, and her plane started the boarding process. Still, a ten-minute delay, giving her thirty minutes to make her connecting flight. That is, if nothing else went wrong.

It seemed to take forever for the plane to taxi the runway, even longer for it to take off. If there was a tailwind, she may have a chance. But at this point, as she sat strapped to her seat in the airplane, there was nothing she could do to make anything go any faster. She closed her eyes and tried to steady her nerves.

No such luck of a tailwind. When the plane finally touched down, she only had fifteen minutes to make her connecting flight—maybe enough if she ran, and nothing else slowed her down along the way.

Miranda stood in line, waiting to disembark from what felt like a tin can trap. Right before she screamed in frustration, the line moved. Disaster averted. She tried to slow her breathing but couldn't ignore the *thump, thump* of her heart beating hard in her chest. She began to wonder if this was what a heart attack felt like.

Ten minutes until departure. Not ten minutes until *boarding*. Ten minutes until *departure*. She gave it her all, but as she reached the departure area, she saw the gate close. She saw the plane slowly back up, and as she ran, for the second time that day, Miranda Morris's heel caught in the corner of the carpet, this time sending her down on one knee. No one was there to catch her while she fell this time. But someone was there to see it and help her up.

Smiley Pete. Again. Seriously? Miranda stared at the man who helped her up, with that same damn grin on his face.

His voice was the first to break the silence. "We have to stop meeting this way." He dusted off her trench coat and handed it to her. Miranda shook her head slowly back and forth. She allowed a small smile to creep on her lips for the first time that day. Because, honestly, if she didn't laugh, she would most definitely cry. The small smile turned into a chuckle and then an outright belly laugh. Before long, she realized that as he stood in front of her with a perplexed smile on his face, she had tears streaming down her face.

She wiped her face with the back of her hand and tried her best to compose herself. Taking a deep breath, she stuck her hand out and said, "Miranda Morris. Nice to meet you."

And, as it turned out, his name was *not* Smiley Pete. Grabbing her hand with both of his, he returned the greeting. "James Barnett. And the pleasure is all mine." Remembering himself, James dropped Miranda's hand with a look of concern. "You were obviously in a hurry. I'll let you go."

"No," she smiled in defeat, "I missed my connection. I'm sure I'll be here for a while."

As it turned out, James was headed home to Washington, DC, and had a two-hour layover. As soon as Miranda found another flight, she realized that she wasn't going anywhere soon either.

It took this major change in her carefully planned schedule to bring her out of the headspace she had occupied all day. When Miranda found James again, she didn't let the opportunity pass her by. "I'm really surprised to see you here."

He gave her a look that said, "Yeah, no kidding."

"What I meant is that I figured you were a local with an inside track on Masterson. In fact, I thought that perhaps your last name might have been 'Masterson.'" It made her feel better to assume nepotism played a role in anyone beating her out of an account.

James cocked his head and narrowed his eyes as he looked at her. "Really? So you couldn't imagine that someone else may have been more suited for this account than you?" Before she could answer, he gave a wry smile and began to laugh as he said, "Well, neither did I. I did my homework, and let me tell you, I was more than a little concerned the more that I learned about you and your firm."

Now it was Miranda's turn to narrow her eyes. "I don't follow. You think I would have been better suited for the account?"

"Don't get me wrong," he said. "I know the capabilities of my firm, and we're a great fit for Masterson. But I actually didn't even know about the account until early last week. If it wasn't for my connection, I wouldn't have had enough time to do all of the legwork necessary to even start a conversation with Masterson."

Miranda was irritated and was certain her tone betrayed this fact. "So, you're telling me that your *connection* did all of your legwork and you got to saunter into Masterson's office and pitch someone else's work as your own, and then *you* walked out with the signed deal?"

Holding up his hand as if to stop the barrage of words that poured from Miranda's mouth, he said, "Now, let me stop you right there. My firm did their due diligence and we are a solid team. We didn't hand in anyone else's work."

Seeing that she had quite possibly put her foot in her mouth, Miranda stopped and sighed. "Okay then, why don't you tell me how you did what you did?"

"Simple," he said. "I asked."

"You asked? Come on. You can't be serious."

"Listen, Miranda, I live my life on a few simple principles. And honestly, they haven't steered me wrong yet. First, the rules. There are no rules!"

Was this guy for real? Miranda wondered, but she could tell that he believed what he was saying, so there must be something to it. And, after all, he did score the Masterson account.

"I exercise my Ask muscle on a daily basis," he said with a gleam in his eye.

"Your what?" she asked.

"You heard me, my Ask muscle."

"Okay, how do you exercise this mystery muscle that I've never heard of?" Miranda was game now. She reasoned that this was more entertaining than reading a dry book on building your business acumen.

James continued, "My Ask muscle. It's the thing that I exercise when I put myself out there. When I need help, I ask for it. And I listen to other people when they need help with something. I remember names. Sometimes I use business cards to trigger my memory. Sometimes I connect the dots by remembering where I saw the person and what was going on when I first met them. Honestly, I'm genuinely interested in other people, and I think this rubs off on the people around me."

Miranda nodded her head. Not too hard yet, and nothing she hadn't done in the past. Although, it was very hard for her to ask for anything when she needed it. She made a mental note of this.

"I'm naturally pretty curious about people. And I don't collect what I learn only to use the knowledge for myself. I pass it along whenever I can. I have too much going on in my own life to hold onto things like that." As they sat talking, Miranda was an eager student and hung on every word that James said. James cleared his throat and continued. "I'm optimistic and like to see the best in people. I guess that's why I'm often a 'go-to' person. And I live on the principle that it's not who I know, but who knows me. You never know when relationships can come in handy."

Ah, so there it was. James had mentioned a connection who had given him the inside track to Masterson. "So tell me about this connection and how it helped you get the Masterson account." Not that it would make any difference to her now, but Miranda was genuinely interested.

James shrugged. "Really, it's nothing big. I had a client years ago, and even though he doesn't use me anymore, I send business his way every now and then."

Miranda was a bit shocked. "So you send business to someone who doesn't even give you his business anymore? I have to admit, I don't think I would waste my time on a relationship like that."

It was James's turn to chuckle. "Really? My business pipeline has been running a little dry recently, so when I saw him, I used my Ask muscle. I told him what I was looking for, and it just so happened that he knew someone at Masterson. I'd say the time I spent sending him business has paid off for me tenfold."

Ouch. He was right. "Okay, so what's so special about this guy? How did he know about Masterson? It doesn't sound like he's in tight with the big boys if you have to throw him bones every now and then."

"Nah, he's a good guy, and he takes care of his relationships."

Miranda snickered again. "Except he's not your client anymore." She paused, letting that sentence hang in the air.

Coming to the rescue of his friend, James shook his head. "You've got it all wrong. Simon didn't renew his contract with my firm a few years back so that he could help his baby sister get started with her own consulting business. And he's doing what he loves. Although a printing company wouldn't be my first choice."

For the second time that day, the world faded to black, and the sound of Miranda's heartbeat thudded in her ears. She knew exactly who the client with the "in" was. And she knew his little sister too. What a fool she had been!

Sensing that her time was up, Miranda shook her head free of thoughts and stood. As she said her goodbyes, she leaned over and extended her hand. James grinned and grasped her hand, shaking it with both of his. "I didn't realize that so much time had gone by. You don't want to miss your connection again."

A smile crept on her lips and Miranda replied, "No, I think I've missed too many connections already. I most certainly am not going to miss another."

Taking her leave, Miranda walked to her gate to start the second leg of her journey. When she settled into her seat, she began to reflect on the last couple of hours. She couldn't be upset with her brother for giving the lead of a lifetime to someone else. She had never asked for his help and certainly never allowed him to give her any unsolicited advice. She was quite certain, in fact, that he had no idea she was even up for the Masterson account.

However, this did lead her to reconsider how she conducted herself and her business. Thinking back, there were so many lost opportunities, and all because she didn't want to ask anyone for help. She also didn't offer her help to anyone else. In the past, she now realized, she had hung onto her knowledge and her contacts with a stingy miser's grip.

Things were going to change. Things had to change. She knew this, knew that there was no other way for growth. She and her colleagues would be spinning their wheels otherwise. And she was not willing to allow that to happen.

So, she thought, where do I begin? As she sat on the plane, Miranda took out a pad of paper and pen and started a list that, she hoped, would transform her world. By the time she disembarked, Miranda clutched the completed list in her hand. She knew the knowledge she had been so freely given that afternoon would prove even more lucrative than the Masterson deal ever would have been.

How to Avoid Missing Connections

Step 1: Look people in the eye. People who open doors for you, serve your meals, take your payments at cash registers. Ask them their names. Make them feel as important as they are. Miranda knew that this wasn't a major thing, but she realized how self-focused she had become and felt like this could be a small step to stop looking inward and be more aware of those around her.

Step 2: Remember that people have connections that extend past the network you are aware of. To really do this thing right, she reckoned, you have to be a bridge to all of the "worlds" in which you have your feet. Miranda had a habit of thinking inside of the box, never considering that the people she knew had relationships that extended from what was right in front of her. Her brother's connection with Masterson, for instance.

Step 3: Be curious and dig deeper. Not everything is what it first appears to be. This was a lesson that she already knew and tried to remember. Sometimes her clients asked for what they thought they wanted. But when she dug a little deeper, she could see that the solutions to their problems were completely different from what they initially asked for.

Step 4: Don't be afraid to say "I don't know." You may not know something initially, but you do know how to find out. Slow down and think things through. Miranda knew that she could use some improvement in this area. She was always so quick to say she couldn't help. She was also quick to say that she didn't need help. This brought her to step five.

Step 5: Don't be afraid of "the ask." Miranda vowed to listen to the asks made of her and to ask when she needed help. She knew that to do this, she needed to make way for the invitation by being more present when she was with other people. Because honestly, it doesn't take that much time to help…or to be helped.

Step 6: Follow through. Period. Relationships, she was beginning to realize, are important. And you have to do what you say you will do to gain the trust of those around you.

Step 7: Recognize it's not who you know but who knows you. She and her brother knew one another, but he really didn't know what she needed and vice versa, simply because she didn't allow it. She was going to work on changing this as soon as she could. Not for the promise of any more business, but because she recognized something in herself that she did not like. And the beauty of it all was that she could change that any time she wanted.

Step 8: Start exercising your Ask muscle daily. Miranda knew that it was going to take a great deal of practice and, like any out-of-shape muscle, it wasn't going to be easy at first.

Sometimes, she mused, you have to lose big to really gain big. Stepping off the plane, Miranda pulled her phone out of her bag and dialed her brother's number. As she waited for him to answer, she felt herself grinning, the same grin James had that had annoyed her so. Now I'm Smiley Pete, she realized with a chuckle.

Case Studies

I suppose there are many different reasons that may motivate a person to undertake the writing of a book. And this was true for me. Honestly, the reasons are so numerous that I do not know where to begin. Perhaps it was my lifelong friend Terri Donohue, who tells me every time we get together, "You cannot make this stuff up. You need to write a book!" I'm not certain if this was the kind of book she was talking about, but there are some things you *do not* want to put into print, my friend!

Mostly, though, I feel like I've stumbled upon a bit of magic through no doing of my own, other than being myself. As I mentioned in the beginning of this book, I was named one of Philadelphia's top 101 connectors. When I first heard that my name had made it on that prestigious list, I had no idea what I'd done to earn the moniker.

I think we tend to assume that everyone operates the same way that we do. As I dug deeper, I found that this was not the case. I had always been genuinely interested in other people. But thanks to the fact that I kept a rather busy schedule, I couldn't afford to be a "collector" of relationships. So out of necessity, I became a "connector" with my relationships. And because I was able to express myself in a way that other people seemed to find both entertaining and informative, I started talking to anyone who wanted to listen about how they could become connectors as well.

Fast-forward to almost ten years later, and I have received hundreds of e-mails from people who followed my advice and saw huge changes in their own lives. Like Miranda in the short fictional piece you just read, they became more intentional about how they were relating to others around them.

Honestly, this book was written to honor the relationships that I have formed throughout the years, honor my fellow connectors, and tell you that you can do it too. It just takes a little bit of exercise to get your Ask muscle into shape. Don't believe me that big things are possible when you simply ask? Well, I've chosen a few stories from the stacks I have on my virtual desk to show you just how easy it is!

Family Ties

Don't ever discount the relationships you already have. Like Miranda's brother in the story, sometimes those closest to you may hold the key to unlock potential connections that could launch you farther than you could ever imagine.

I have a large family, and nothing makes me happier than being able to help the people that I love fulfill their dreams. One such person is my nephew, Matt Alba. As a senior at Temple University, he was reluctant to accept any outside help and was content to stay in the safe confines of the academic world in which he had found so much success. But the day always comes when you have to leave the nest and venture out into the world. And that day finally came for Matt, who was a journalism major. What a highly competitive field! Let's just say that sometimes resumes can sit in an inbox and never see the light of day.

When Matt asked me whether I could help him find an internship in the broadcasting industry, I was able to connect him with a contact I had, Lauren Bacigalupi. Lauren was someone that I'd met while filming a client who was receiving a big award. When I reached out to Lauren and asked her for guidance, she graciously agreed to sit down with Matt for an informational interview. The connection they made was instantaneous, and her advice resulted in an internship for Matt at NBC10. Through further connections he made in the NBC10 family, he got his first job in journalism at NBC40 in Atlantic City, New Jersey.

Matt has gone on to become a reporter for NBC2 in Charleston, South Carolina. And while he definitely traded up in the weather, he will never forget the connections he made in his hometown of Philadelphia. And just like Miranda, if Matt hadn't asked me for guidance, I would never have known to talk to the people I was connected to on his behalf.

When Connectors Connect

I love it when I get the chance to speak and walk away from the engagement with a new friend. That certainly happened with my friend Susan McDonald. She attended a dinner where I spoke about being a connector. When Susan arrived, she had a ton on her mind. Her son, who was finishing up college, had been through the process of interviewing for his dream job with NFL Films. Unfortunately, he had just been given the news that he didn't get the job. Who hasn't been in that position before? And I'm sure it's even harder when it happens to your child and you feel like don't have an ounce of control over the outcome.

It's no wonder that Susan's hand shot up when I asked people to start exercising their Ask muscles at the end of my presentation. Susan explained her son's dilemma. Since he didn't get his dream job, he needed to find an internship opportunity, and quick.

It just so happened that I had a connection that opened an opportunity for Susan's son, Ryan, to be on staff in the Eagles Game Day PR department. Susan and Ryan had put in a good amount of legwork before we even met, so there is a chance that Ryan would have eventually made this connection anyway. But Susan says the moral of the story is that if she had never made the ask the night we met, her son would not have been in that position.

As a disclaimer, Susan is a seasoned connector, and when she made her ask, it was with a well-developed Ask muscle. She and Ryan were flexible and tenacious and never assumed a passive role. As a result, Susan says that her son gained an invaluable life lesson.

eXude

My firm has been a longtime client of a company called eXude for our benefit needs. When Michelle

Tepper, president of Specialty Products Division, contacted me about speaking at an intimate breakfast meeting they were holding for some clients, I jumped at the chance. A connector loves to connect!

When I have speaking engagements I will oftentimes have colleagues of mine attend with me to take notes or help with the facilitation of the engagement. My colleagues Patty Cook and Meg Byrne attended with me for that particular event. Imagine my delight when Patty was able to connect with not one but two of the attendees when they exercised their Ask muscles. One woman in particular needed help making her LinkedIn profile more exciting. So when she raised her hand and made the ask, Patty, having experience with this, offered to meet and help her. Another woman said she and her husband would soon be moving to Cleveland and didn't know anyone in that area. Again Patty had a connection, a friend who lived in Cleveland and was well connected. Patty made the connection between the two women, and if they're anything like their friend Patty, they connected.

Events and speaking engagements are kind of like seeds. They're one small part in the whole grand scheme of things. But what comes from them over time can spread and be farther reaching than what that one small event or engagement ever was.

From speaking to Michelle, I have heard that what has taken place after the engagement has been like a domino effect. Word is spreading and people are connecting. There really was an energy in the room that day. People were excited to talk about connections that were made. eXude continues to connect their clients and others by hosting different events around the city of Philadelphia. In fact, my colleague Patty (what a connector she is!) was invited to attend a happy hour that eXude hosted for professional women in the city. Patty brought our colleague Meg with her, thus helping Meg fulfill her 2015 goal of being a better connector. See? Tiny seeds sprouting roots and growing into plants.

Dow Linc80 Series

One speaking engagement I am particularly proud of yielded some impressive connections. I was approached by Dow Chemical to present at one of their prestigious *Linc80* events. This event brings together Dow Chemical's "high potentials," both seasoned and inexperienced employees who show a high aptitude in the field. This particular series' theme was "Connecting"...right up my alley!

At some point in every presentation I give, I ask random audience members to stand up and exercise their Ask muscles. What I found when I spoke to this large and very professional gathering was that they were accustomed to a more technical presentation. This kind of discussion was new for this group, and it took a while for the crowd to get warmed up to me. But once they did get warmed up, boy did they get moving!

There's absolutely nothing wrong with making an ask in your professional life. In fact, I highly recommend it. But there are so many different facets of life, so many places where we could use a little extra something. I think it's pretty safe to say that as much as many of us may enjoy our jobs, it's called "work" for a reason. Why not make it a more comfortable place to be by creating some lasting connections that reflect who we truly are?

That's just what this particular Dow group did. Once they made themselves vulnerable, they started making more personal asks, from people just moving to the area who needed to be shown the lay of the land to people asking for help with home improvement projects. These people let down their guards and simply asked.

One of the organizers, Fallyn Flaherty-Earp, mentioned that at Dow, connections are key, but acknowledged that there is not often time for connection on a personal level. After my connector event, several women in attendance started a monthly happy hour because of the lessons they learned. What a success! Because of exercising their Ask muscles, they have created a sense of community that adds a personal element to their work. Fallyn says that people learned that it was okay to ask for things, and since then, they've seen a change in how long it takes to get what they need done, done. Imagine that—a personal connection can pay off at work!

I'll never forget sharing with another of the *Linc80* event's organizers, Jennifer Sandusky, what I called a belated birthday gift. I received an e-mail from a young man who was working the event as an intern, and through my conversation with him I learned that he had an ask, so when I gave him the floor, he took it. Instead of telling you what happened in his life, I'd like to share with you the e-mail he sent to me. You just cannot beat the power of a connector!

Hello Ms. Dunleavy,

I wanted to send you an email in regards to the Dow Linc80 conference in which you spoke at last month. I was the young man who you connected with the entire group of participants. I wanted to thank you and express my gratitude. You have truly helped me to embark upon my future goals. You have made a big impact upon my future career and really helped me to begin networking here at Dow.

I am now using many of the connections that you have helped me to develop to apply to Dow's Commercial Development Program upon my college graduation next Spring. This is a six month rotational sales program for recent graduates. I am also developing connections in Dow's Electronic Materials department as I had said my interests were. People are very eager to help when I tell them my specific goals as you had said.

I hope you realize the impact you have had and keep changing lives!

Sincerely, Mike Witowski

Women2Women

Another organization that has become dear to my heart is Women2Women, managed by the Greater Reading Chamber of Commerce. I have had the opportunity to speak to this group of women twice, and neither time disappointed. The first was in November of 2014, and I spoke about being a connector. The second time I spoke to this group was almost exactly a year later and I spoke about...being a connector!

I am not a one-trick pony and told the organizers I had other things I could talk about. "Are you sure?" I asked. Did their audience really want to hear the same thing twice? They assured me they did and I acquiesced, and I am glad I did. Some amazing connections came from both of my speaking engagements with this dynamic group of women.

This organization's mission statement says that they are passionate about "creating connections, gaining knowledge, opening doors and building strategic alliances." They state that their "goal is to create more women leaders in Berks County by providing a forum where women from diverse backgrounds can learn, share ideas and mentor each other." Talk about being passionate about being connectors. No wonder they didn't mind hearing me talk about making connections twice! So many amazing connections were made both years in a row. And, true to the connectors that these women are, they couldn't wait to tell me about them.

In attendance both years was Regina Rinehimer, who sat on the board of a nonprofit shelter for women and their children called Mary's Shelter. The organization had acquired a large building that was formerly a marine and naval training facility. When the shelter was finally able to occupy the building, they needed all sorts of help to get the place up and running. So, when Regina attended my connector event, she had a thousand things on her mind. And she did not hesitate to exercise her Ask muscle when it came time to do so.

When Regina walked out of the room that day, she not only acquired two to three hundred dollars generously donated by members in attendance, she, in effect, launched a campaign to spread the word about something that was so dear to her heart.

A woman in attendance offered her local weekly TV show as a commercial of sorts for the shelter. When Regina appeared on the show, she was able to announce to the community what Mary's Shelter was about to embark on. In addition to the TV show, an employee from a local business offered to make Mary's Shelter their Christmas charity that year. This business held clothing and food drives, among other things.

Another success story that came out of this group of women comes from Kim Rivera, executive director of Girls on the Run, Berks County. Kim's chapter of Girls on the Run was in need of volunteers for a 5K event they were participating in. She made the ask when she had the floor and had several people express interest in volunteering. Others committed to spread the word in their organizations. From her initial ask, Kim still has a team of two sisters that continue to volunteer.

Probably one of the most exciting connections to come from the 2015 Women2Women event involved Dee Mathis with the American Cancer Society. This was the fourth year that she had been involved with a Santa letter writing campaign at Christmas to benefit Relay for Life and the American Cancer Society. Dee needed quite a few volunteers for this project to write letters, Santas to call children, and even people to dress up like Santa to give these children a special Christmas treat.

Dee got up when the time came to exercise her Ask muscle and, because of this, received an outpouring of support she could never have imagined.

That day, she walked away with the business cards of twenty people who showed interest in the letter writing campaign. When the night of the event came, around twenty-five volunteers showed up to write letters, many coming because Dee exercised her Ask muscle. A total of 233 letters were written that night. But I think it's safe to say that the power of these connections will endure for years to come.

The bottom line is this: Regina, Kim, and Dee would have been able to eventually spread the word about their individual endeavors, but if they hadn't stepped up when they had the floor, it would have been much slower going. When we are more conscious about trying to make connections, we can recognize the opportunities that have been right in front of our faces. It really is so simple; you just have to ask.

Pennsylvania Conference for Women

Finally, I'd like to share with you the conference I spoke at where I realized that I had really hit on something special. The Pennsylvania Conference for Women takes place in my hometown of Philadelphia, Pennsylvania, at the Pennsylvania Convention Center. There is always something special about a hometown crowd, and it was certainly true on this occasion.

I felt blessed to be asked to be a part of such an empowering event. As a breakout session speaker for this event, one of the largest women's conferences in the nation, I was joining a long and impressive group of speakers. Let's just say that my role was only a little smaller than Hillary Clinton's the year that she spoke.

In preparation for the event, I was told that I would be speaking to an intimate group of people in a smaller-sized room. What is it that they say about the best-laid plans? Yeah, that was very true in this particular case. When I walked into a very large and imposing room, chairs spread from one corner to the other, I thought, "Houston, we've got a problem!"

So, I did what I always do. I put my big girl pants on and went to work. This change in plans forced me to think outside of the box. The impersonal room in reality caused me to be more intimate with my audience. When I asked for people to exercise their Ask muscles, I was the one who really got the workout! I ran from table to table, raised hand to raised hand, with my small lavalier microphone asking people to speak into my lapel. And yes, I did get some strange looks. But the room was abuzz, and people caught the enthusiasm that I'd had to muster myself only moments before the beginning of my presentation.

I heard later that people were fascinated by how more than one person raised their hands to help when others asked. It was inspiring to see that you could ask for something and people would fill the order so quickly. That is the true power of connecting.

Cheryl Pompeo, now a colleague of mine, was in attendance that day. At the time, she was the executive director of the Arthritis Foundation's eastern Pennsylvania chapter. When she raised her hand, she told us she was looking to find someone to fill an open position on their board. Filling a board position with the right person can sometimes take quite a while, but not on this day. A woman in attendance raised her hand and offered her services. As it turned out, she was an appropriate choice for many reasons and subsequently joined the board. This is not an unusual outcome. As I've said, I have stacks of stories on my virtual desk to support that fact.

As for me? Even though I did not have that particular ask at that particular time, I personally ended up with connections that day that would evolve into the onboarding of two of my valued colleagues in my firm. See, anyone can connect at any time. You just need to be aware of what is going on around you.

Practice Makes Perfect

The biggest takeaway you should have from all of these stories is that you don't need to go it alone. The poet John Donne was right: no man is an island. Whether you grew up knowing how to exercise your Ask muscle or not, it's something that anyone can do. And the more you do it, the easier it becomes and the better the results.

Be intentional about what you need and about what you have to offer. When did "networking" become a verb, anyway? It's not. "Connect," however, is a verb. Be a connector who is intent on making connections and connecting people, not someone who leverages their network. See where I'm going with this? We cannot take for granted the humanity in our relationships, whether business or professional.

Be that go-to person with your feet in both worlds, bridging gaps and rewarding the faith that others have placed in you. Position yourself for meaningful connections. Because that, my friend, is what makes the world go round.

Listen to others around you.

When we close our mouths and open our ears, it's amazing what can happen.

Use a person's name when speaking to them.

I have a knack for remembering names and faces, but not everyone has that particular strength. Find ways to jog your memory. Ask them how to spell it ("Is that Michele with one 'l' or two?"). Write a name down. Think up a rhyme. Repeat the person's name back to them when they say it to you. Whatever it takes, a small way to make people feel valued is to speak to them as if you are already friends.

Ask questions to learn more about others.

Remember that it's not always about you. (In fact, it rarely is!) Be curious and interested in other people. It's amazing what you can learn when you ask a few questions. Don't forget that relationships are a two-way street.

Don't keep thoughts to yourself (sometimes).

People aren't mind readers and can't help if you don't tell them what you need. Even little things. If nothing else, it does help with relationship building.

Be willing to be open.

This is a hard thing. Vulnerability is not easy, but just like exercising your Ask muscle, it gets easier the more you do it.

Do what you say.

Follow-through is key, and to be a valued advisor, you cannot let things wither and die on the vine. When you step up and say you'll help, do just that.

Always take the commercial when you have the floor.

How often do we really get the chance to have the floor? Not often. So, when you do, step out and step up. Don't let that opportunity pass you by. You may not get another chance.

Express gratitude!

Say thank you often and mean it. When someone asks you for something, consider it a gift (because it is).

My Ask of You

And now, I'm going to end by modeling the behaviors that I teach— ASKING! First, I'd ask that you stop and think of how you need help (or can offer it) and who you can connect with to make it happen. Next, I'd ask that you encourage someone to read this book— whether a friend, family member, or colleague. You can be the connector that helps them become a connector. They may even become one of your "go-to" connections when you need help. Finally, I'd ask that you keep in touch with me— tell me your success stories— who knows, you may be in my second book! My email is **ExerciseYourAskMuscle@gmail.com**. Please use it!

With gratitude, Nancy

NANCY DUNLEAVY
Founder & CEO,
Dunleavy & Associates

Nancy Dunleavy is the founder and CEO of Dunleavy & Associates, a woman-owned business founded in 2001 to empower charitable organizations to achieve their fullest potential. Nancy describes herself as a "rainmaker" and an "extraordinary talent scout" having recruited phenomenal clients, colleagues and collaborators. An inspirational public speaker, Nancy is frequently engaged to speak on topics of philanthropy, governance, women in leadership, and management of charitable organizations.

Nancy was named by LEADERSHIP Philadelphia

as one of Philadelphia's "Top 101 Connectors" and by the Philadelphia Business Journal as one of the 25 Women of Distinction in 2006 and one of the top 100 women-owned businesses in 2011. She brings an extensive network of contacts and relationships to clients of the firm. Her ability to "cross industry sectors" has been cited as one of the characteristics of true connectors and she is successful in engaging collaborations between and among the educational community, the political community, the nonprofit community and the corporate community.

Her career as an entrepreneur was preceded by more than twenty years in the healthcare business, as a senior financial manager and hospital administrator. Prior to launching Dunleavy & Associates, she served for ten years as Chief Financial Officer and then two years as the Senior Vice President for Corporate Development for Friends Hospital and Behavioral Health System.

A committed and engaged community leader, Nancy contributes her time and talent to several organizations and non-profit Boards of Directors in the region. She chairs the Gwynedd-Mercy College Board of Trustees, and serves on the LEADERSHIP Philadelphia Board of Directors, the Greater Philadelphia Chamber of Commerce Board of Directors, the Valley Forge Convention and Visitors Bureau Board of Trustees, where she serves as Treasurer, and the the North Penn Community Health Foundation Board of Directors where she serves as vice-chair. A 2006 alumna of the Anne B. Anstine Excellence in Public Service Series, Nancy accepted a 2012 appointment to the Whitpain Township Planning Commission.